False Alarms

by Steve Cole
Illustrated by Bill Ledger

In this story ...

Evan
(Flex)

Evan is super stretchy! He can stretch his body in any direction. He once stretched his arms all the way around Hero Academy.

Pip
(Boost)

Pip is super strong! She can lift up really heavy weights, like boulders. She once lifted a skyscraper.

Chapter 1:
Superheroes of the Day!

Evan and Pip felt very proud as they stood in the Head's office.

"As a reward for working hard," said the Head, "I am making you Superheroes of the Day!"

Pip turned to Evan. "That means if the police are too busy today, we get to help out!"

"The Grand White Gemstone has just arrived at the Lexis City Gallery," said the Head. "It's the rarest jewel in the world, so the police will be busy patrolling nearby."

Evan gasped. "Every villain around must want that gemstone."

At that moment, a shrill, bleeping sound came from a screen, and Police Commissioner Jordan's face appeared.

"I need your help, heroes," said Police Commissioner Jordan.

"What's happened?" asked the Head.

"A man dressed as a clown is taking money from Lexis City Bank," said the Commissioner.

"We'll investigate straight away," replied the Head.

"This is a job for Boost and Flex!" Evan cried. "To the bank!"

Chapter 2:
A cross clown

Evan and Pip changed into their superhero costumes and became Flex and Boost. Then they raced at top speed to the bank.

Flex spotted the clown through a window. He was holding a big bag of money.

"There he is!" Flex cried.

Boost smashed through the doors.

"Stop right there!" she ordered.

Flex stretched out his arm, knocking the money-bag to the floor.

"What are you doing?" said the clown angrily. "This money belongs to the circus! Our clown cars have flat tyres so the boss sent me out to buy new ones."

The bank manager hurried across.

"What's happened to my door?" he asked crossly.

Boost's cheeks turned as red as the clown's nose. "Sorry—"

"And why are you bothering my customers?" demanded the bank manager, scowling. "I should call the police!"

Flex and Boost left in a hurry.

"He doesn't know that it was the police that called *us*," Flex sighed. "We jumped to the wrong conclusion about that clown."

Chapter 3:
Crime wave?

The Head was frowning when Boost and Flex got back.

"Sorry," said Boost quickly. "The clown was innocent but we didn't give him a chance to explain."

Flex unclipped his Superhero of the Day badge and tried to give it back.

"Keep it," said the Head. "No real harm was done. I've arranged for the door of the bank to be fixed." He smiled. "When the bank manager saw your costumes, he thought you'd come from a rival circus!"

Suddenly, the screen bleeped, and the Commissioner's face appeared again.

"A suspected thief has been seen sneaking in and out of windows in the Cloudscratch Skyscraper," she said.

"We're on our way!" cried Boost.

Boost and Flex raced to the skyscraper. High above, someone was standing on a platform, holding a bucket.

"The thief!" cried Boost. "That bucket must be full of his stolen loot. Flex, get up there!"

Flex stretched his legs like an ultra-long ladder, and zoomed up towards the intruder.

On his way up, Flex accidentally knocked the platform. The man slipped and his bucket landed on his head.

"Ha!" Flex exclaimed. "Caught you in the act, thief!"

Boost cheered from the pavement.

"Thief?" the man said, trying to pull the bucket off his head. "I'm a window cleaner!"

Back on the ground, Flex groaned. "I can't believe we made another mistake."

"At least you got down from the platform before the window cleaner could pull off the bucket and see you," Boost said.

Even so, Flex felt rotten.

The friends hurried back to Hero Academy, where the Head was waiting for them.

"Another false alarm," Flex explained.

"Most peculiar," the Head replied. "Never mind. Commissioner Jordan has called again. A large, mysterious hole has appeared in Halfway Hill, at the edge of the city. You must investigate. This time, be careful – it could be another false alarm."

"We will," Boost promised. "Come on, Flex!"

Chapter 4:
The hole truth

The sun was going down as Flex and Boost reached the hole in the hillside.

"It's probably just a big animal burrow," said Flex. "Maybe we should go. You heard the Head – it could just be another false alarm."

Boost shook her head. "But what if it isn't?" She took a small torch from the pouch on her belt and climbed into the hole. "Let's explore!"

"This tunnel goes on for a long way," said Boost.

"A very long way," Flex agreed. "It's leading us underneath the city!"

The tunnel finally sloped upwards, and then they began to see some light. Boost and Flex stopped at the end of the tunnel and peered out. They could see a magnificent jewel shining in the centre of a room.

"That's the Grand White Gemstone!" Boost cried. "We're in the Lexis City Gallery!"

Flex gasped as he spotted a familiar, fiendish figure. It was Ray Ranter, arch-enemy of Hero Academy, on the other side of the room. He was giving his bunny-wunnies orders.

"He must be here to steal the jewel!" Boost said.

Ranter scowled at them. "What are you doing here? You were supposed to be busy. I phoned the Commissioner enough times."

Ray Ranter

NUMBER 1 MOST WANTED VILLAIN

Catchphrase: Heroes are zeroes!

Hobbies: stamp collecting. He would love nothing more than to have a set of Ranter stamps.

Likes: white rooms, white suits, turnips (because they're white).

Dislikes: all colours, and raspberries (because they're hairy, and raspberry stains are impossible to remove from white suits).

Beware! He created robotic rabbits – bunny-wunnies – to help him carry out his dastardly plans.

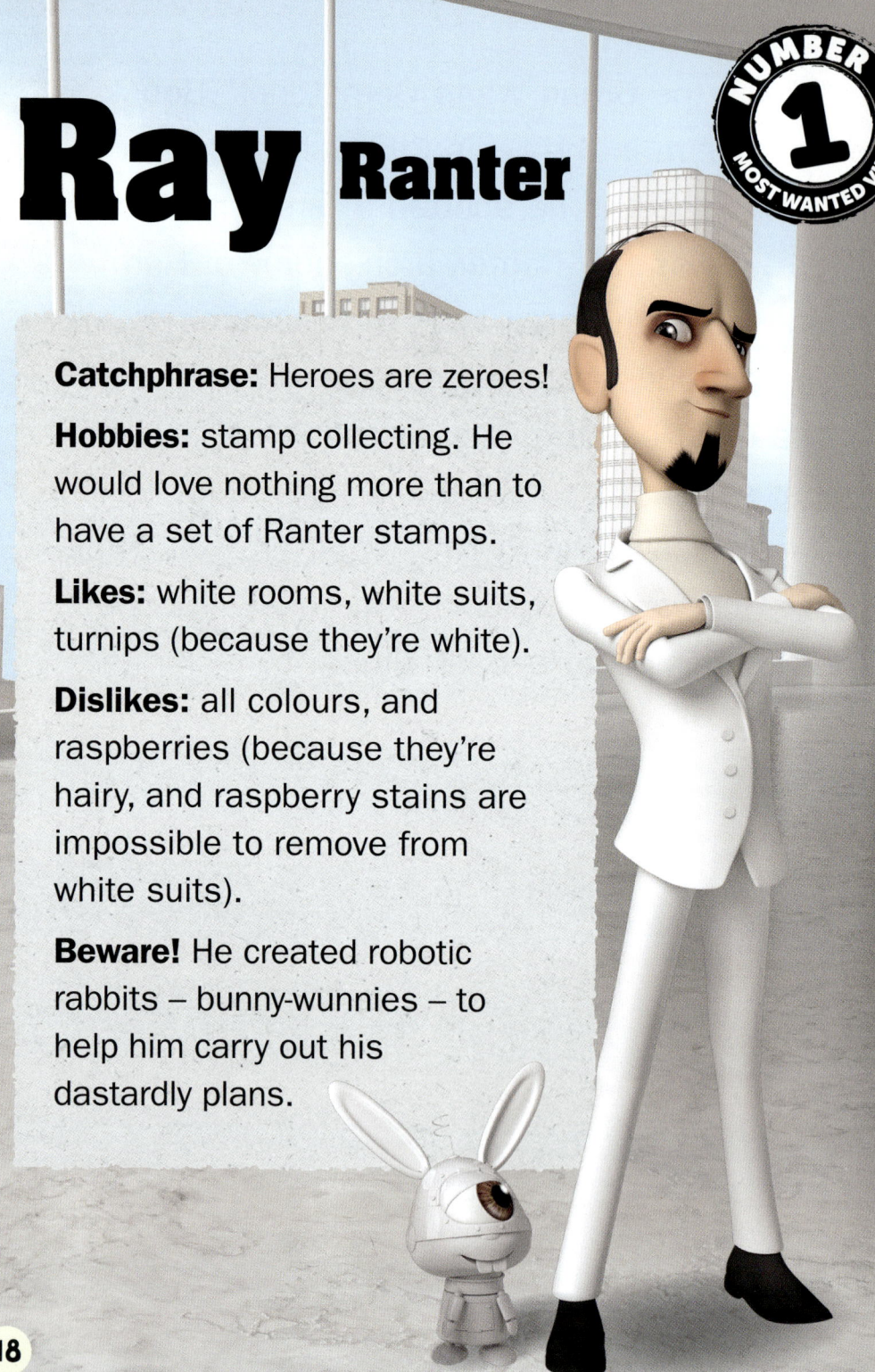

"So *you* made the false reports!" said Flex.

"That's right," Ranter replied, looking smug.

"Well, someone else reported your hole in Halfway Hill and called the police," said Boost. "I suppose you thought you could tunnel in here and just snatch the gemstone?"

"Yes," Ranter snarled, "and you won't stop me!"

Ranter pulled a small, yellow gadget from his pocket.

"I have taken control of the gallery's security systems," he gloated. "I hear that the intruder catcher is quite effective. Shall we find out?"

He pressed a button and a thick, steel cage shot up from floor to ceiling. Boost and Flex were trapped.

Ranter grabbed the jewel, then laughed and waved. "Farewell!"

"Oh no you don't," said Flex. He stretched a super-long arm through the bars of the cage, grabbed the yellow gadget and hit the button. The cage slid back down.

Ranter ran towards the tunnel.

Boost stamped her foot on the floor with incredible strength. The shockwave was like an earthquake! It knocked Ranter to the floor.

As Ranter fell, the Grand White Gemstone flew out of his hand. In a flash, Flex stretched out and caught it.

Boost pressed another button on the yellow gadget. All the gallery's alarms went off at once.

"That should bring the police!" Boost said, grinning.

With a bellow of rage, Ranter dived into the tunnel.

"After him!" Flex yelled.

Boost and Flex began to follow, but Ranter's bunny-wunnies were furiously filling the tunnel with earth behind them.

"He's getting away!" cried Boost.

"We'll catch him another day." Flex replied.

Flex put the Grand White Gemstone back, and the heroes raced towards the nearest exit.

Back at Hero Academy, the Head smiled at Evan and Pip.

"You really are Superheroes of the Day!" he said. "Now, hopefully Ray Ranter has learned his lesson and there won't be any more false alarms."

"Talking of alarms …" Pip said. "Has the dinner bell gone yet?"

"Good point, Pip," Evan said, rubbing his stomach. "I'm starving!"